EARTH SCIENCE EXPLORERS

DISCOVER!

WHY IS EARTH ROUND?

BY JANE R. DAVIS

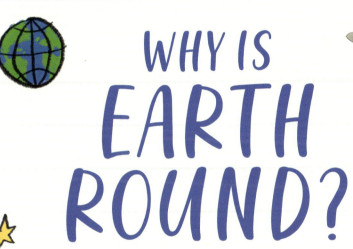

Enslow
PUBLISHING

Please visit our website, www.enslow.com. For a free color catalog of all our high-quality books, call toll free 1-800-398-2504 or fax 1-877-980-4454.

Library of Congress Cataloging-in-Publication Data

Names: Davis, Jane R., author.
Title: Why is Earth round? / Jane R. Davis.
Description: Buffalo, New York : Enslow Publishing, [2026] | Series: Earth science explorers | Includes bibliographical references and index. | Audience: Grades K-1
Identifiers: LCCN 2024061262 (print) | LCCN 2024061263 (ebook) | ISBN 9781978543744 (library binding) | ISBN 9781978543737 (paperback) | ISBN 9781978543751 (ebook)
Subjects: LCSH: Earth (Planet)–Figure–Juvenile literature.
Classification: LCC QB286 .D39 2026 (print) | LCC QB286 (ebook) | DDC 515/.1–dc23/eng/20250116
LC record available at https://lccn.loc.gov/2024061262
LC ebook record available at https://lccn.loc.gov/2024061263

Published in 2026 by
Enslow Publishing
2544 Clinton Street
Buffalo, NY 14224

Copyright © 2026 Enslow Publishing

Designer: Claire Zimmermann
Editor: Kristen Nelson

Photo credits: Cover (girl) Roman Samborskyi/Shutterstock.com, (earth photo) 24K-Production/Shutterstock.com; series art (composition book texture) notebook-texture/Shutterstock.com, (tape) pics five/Shutterstock.com, (doodles and illustrations used throughout) Claire Zimmermann; p. 5 Monkey Business Images/Shutterstock.com; p. 7 Sergey Nivens/Shutterstock.com; p. 9 NASA Goddard Space Flight Center/flickr; p. 11 NetPix/Shutterstock.com; p. 13 yusufdemirci/Shutterstock.com; p. 15 Tatiana_kashko_photo/Shutterstock.com; p. 17 Travelstock by Powerhouse/Shutterstock.com; p. 19 Dario Pena/Shutterstock.com; p. 21 image courtesy of NASA.

All rights reserved. No part of this book may be reproduced in any form without permission in writing from the publisher, except by a reviewer.

Printed in the United States of America

Some of the images in this book illustrate individuals who are models. The depictions do not imply actual situations or events.

CPSIA compliance information: Batch #CSENS26: For further information contact Enslow Publishing, at 1-800-398-2504.

CONTENTS

A Globe 4

Making a Planet 6

Got Gravity? 8

Spin Around 12

Highs and Lows 14

Proof! 16

Study Earth 20

Glossary 22

For More Information 23

Index 24

BOLDFACE WORDS APPEAR IN THE GLOSSARY

A GLOBE

Have you ever seen a globe? This is a **model** of planet Earth. You may have noticed its shape: a sphere, or 3D circle. The word "globe" even means "something round." That's because our Earth is round!

A GLOBE COMMONLY HAS COUNTRIES, RIVERS, OCEANS, AND MORE MARKED ON IT.

MAKING A PLANET

Earth formed **billions** of years ago. It started as matter in space bumping into more matter. The matter joined together. As the **mass** grew bigger, it began to have its own gravity. This pulled in even more space matter.

↑ THE OTHER PLANETS IN OUR SOLAR SYSTEM FORMED IN MUCH THE SAME WAY AS EARTH.

GOT GRAVITY?

Gravity is the **force** that pulls matter toward the center of a planet or star. It's also the force that keeps your feet on the ground and your chair in place. But first, it was important in forming Earth!

THIS IS WHAT EARTH LOOKS LIKE FROM SPACE.

Gravity pulls on all parts of a planet equally. Think of how the spokes on a bicycle wheel **extend** out from the center. That's how gravity pulls. This makes a planet's shape a sphere!

SPIN AROUND

Earth spins around an imaginary straight line called an axis. As it spins, the area around the **equator** has to move just a little bit faster than the rest of the planet. It makes this part of the planet **bulge** just a tiny bit.

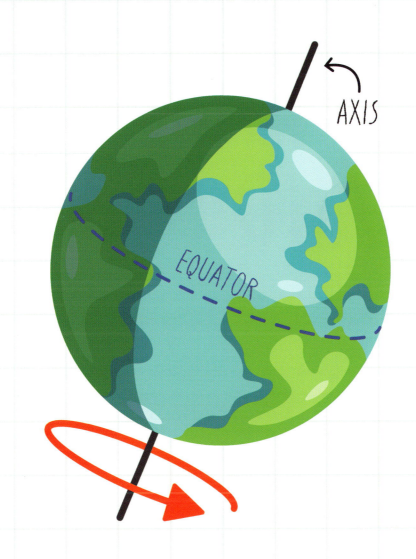

EVEN WITH ITS BULGE, EARTH IS ONE OF THE ROUNDEST PLANETS.

HIGHS AND LOWS

Even though Earth is round, it's not smooth! There are very tall mountains and very deep ocean **trenches** found on Earth. Earth's shape is always changing. The movement of **tectonic plates** is one reason this happens.

MOUNT EVEREST

MOUNT EVEREST IS THE HIGHEST MOUNTAIN ON EARTH FOUND ABOVE SEA LEVEL.

15

PROOF!

Look at the ground under your feet. Does it look rounded to you? It might be hard to believe that Earth is round. There are ways scientists know it is though. First, Earth's shadow on the moon during an eclipse is round.

A **LUNAR** ECLIPSE HAPPENS BECAUSE THE EARTH IS RIGHT BETWEEN THE MOON AND SUN. THIS MAKES EARTH'S SHADOW FALL ON THE MOON.

Look into the distance. Can you see something hundreds of miles away? You can't because Earth is round! Earth itself is in the way of you seeing it. If Earth were flat, you would be able to see very far away on a clear day.

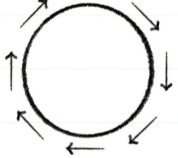

THE PLACE WHERE THE EARTH SEEMS TO MEET THE SKY IS CALLED THE HORIZON. YOU SEE IT BECAUSE OF EARTH'S SHAPE.

19

STUDY EARTH

Scientists are always studying Earth's size, shape, and how gravity affects it. This study is called geodesy. There's so much more to learn about our planet! Would you like to study it yourself someday?

SOMETIMES EARTH IS CALLED THE "BLUE MARBLE" BECAUSE OF ITS SHAPE AND COLOR!

GLOSSARY

billion: 1,000 million, or 1,000,000,000.

bulge: A part that juts out.

equator: An imaginary line around Earth that is the same distance from the North and South Poles.

extend: To stretch out.

force: A push or pull.

lunar: Having to do with the moon.

mass: A large body.

model: A small representation of something.

tectonic plates: One of the moveable masses of rock that create Earth's surface.

trench: A long, narrow hole in the ground.

FOR MORE INFORMATION

BOOKS

Owens, L. L. *Earth.* Mankato, MN: Child's World, 2025.

Wood, Alix. *Zoom Around Planet Earth.* Buffalo, NY: Windmill Books, 2024.

WEBSITES

Earth | NASA Space Place
https://spaceplace.nasa.gov/menu/earth/
Find out all about our planet here.

What Is Gravity? | NASA Space Place
https://spaceplace.nasa.gov/what-is-gravity/en/
Explore the force of gravity!

Publisher's note to educators and parents: Our editors have carefully reviewed these websites to ensure that they are suitable for students. Many websites change frequently, however, and we cannot guarantee that a site's future contents will continue to meet our high standards of quality and educational value. Be advised that students should be closely supervised whenever they access the internet.

INDEX

- axis, 12
- eclipse, 16, 17
- equator, 12
- geodesy, 20
- gravity, 6, 8, 10, 20
- horizon, 19
- moon, 16, 17
- Mount Everest, 15
- planets forming, 6, 7, 8
- space, 6, 8
- tectonic plates, 14